07
09

CITY OF BURBANK
Public Library

SQUARES

AND

COURTYARDS

OTHER BOOKS BY MARILYN HACKER

Selected Poems: 1965–1990

Winter Numbers: Poems

Going Back to the River

Love, Death, and the Changing of the Seasons

Assumptions

Taking Notice

Separations

Presentation Piece

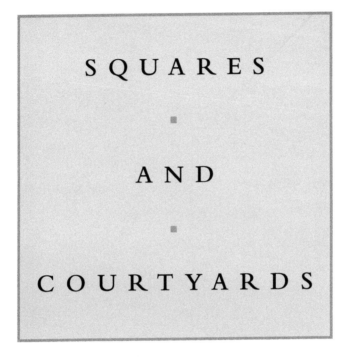

SQUARES

AND

COURTYARDS

Marilyn Hacker

W. W. NORTON & COMPANY

NEW YORK LONDON

For information about permission to reproduce selections from this book,
write to Permissions, W. W. Norton & Company, Inc.,
500 Fifth Avenue, New York, NY 10110

The text of this book is composed in Bembo with the display set in Bembo SemiBold.
Composition by JoAnn Schambier
Manufacturing by The Courier Companies, Inc.
Book design by JAM Design

Library of Congress Cataloging-in-Publication Data

Hacker, Marilyn, 1942–
        Squares and courtyards / Marilyn Hacker.
            p.   cm.
        ISBN 0-393-04830-6
        I. Title.
    PS3558.A28S69   2000
    811'.54—dc21
                                                99-39110
                                                CIP

W. W. Norton & Company, Inc., 500 Fifth Avenue, New York, N.Y. 10110
                        www.wwnorton.com

W. W. Norton & Company Ltd., 10 Coptic Street, London WC1A 1PU

1 2 3 4 5 6 7 8 9 0

For Hayden Carruth

Grateful acknowledgment is given to the journals in which poems in this book originally appeared: *Agni, Ambit, American Poetry Review, The Antioch Review, HEArt, Latin American Literature and Arts, Metre, PN Review, The Paris Review, Ploughshares, Poetry Review, Prairie Schooner, River Styx, Shenandoah, TROIS, TriQuarterly, The Yale Review.*

The following sections of "Paragraphs from a Daybook" first appeared in *Poetry*:

> *Thought thrusts up, homely as a hyacinth*
> *Trace, on a city map, trajectories,*
> *A question-mark in yellow overalls*
> *I was four, in itchy woolen leggings*
> *It's hot for May. The woman hugs the wall*
> *No more Lysol, only lavender*
> *A snapshot, after all, is a cliché*

"Invocation" appeared in the 1998 *Pushcart Prize* anthology. "Again, the River" appeared in *Best American Poetry of 1998*, John Hollander and David Lehman, editors. "The Boy" and "Invocation" appeared in the *Bread Loaf Anthology of Contemporary American Poetry*, Sydney Lea and Stanley Plumly, editors, in 1999. "Squares and Courtyards" received *Prairie Schooner*'s Strousse Award in 1998.

CONTENTS

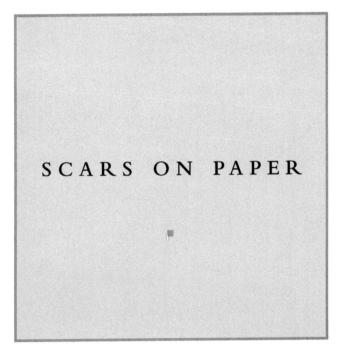

SCARS ON PAPER

THE BOY

Is it the boy in me who's looking out
the window, while someone across the street
mends a pillowcase, clouds shift, the gutter spout
pours rain, someone else lights a cigarette?

(Because he flinched, because he didn't whirl
around, face them, because he didn't hurl
the challenge back—*"Fascists?"*—not *"Faggots"*—*"Swine!"*
he briefly wonders—if he were a girl . . .)
He writes a line. He crosses out a line.

I'll never be a man, but there's a boy
crossing out words: the rain, the linen-mender,
are all the homework he will do today.
The absence and the privilege of gender

confound in him, soprano, clumsy, frail.
Not neuter—neutral human, and unmarked,
the younger brother in the fairy tale
except, boys shouted *"Jew!"* across the park

at him when he was coming home from school.
The book that he just read, about the war,
the partisans, is less a terrible
and thrilling story, more a warning, more

a code, and he must puzzle out the code.
He has short hair, a red sweatshirt. They know

something about him—that he should be proud
of? That's shameful if it shows?

That got you killed in 1942.
In his story, do the partisans
have sons? Have grandparents? Is he a Jew
more than he is a boy, who'll be a man

someday? Someone who'll never be a man
looks out the window at the rain he thought
might stop. He reads the sentence he began.
He writes down something that he crosses out.

SCARS ON PAPER

An unwrapped icon, too potent to touch,
she freed my breasts from the camp Empire dress.
Now one of them's the shadow of a breast
with a lost object's half-life, with as much
life as an anecdotal photograph:
me, Kim and Iva, all stripped to the waist,
hiking near Russian River on June first
'79: Iva's five-and-a-half.
While *she* was almost twenty, wearing black
T-shirts in D.C., where we hadn't met.
You lay your palm, my love, on my flat chest.
In lines alive with what is not regret,
she takes her own path past, doesn't turn back.
Persistently, on paper, we exist.

Persistently, on paper, we exist.
You'd touch me if you could, but you're, in fact,
three thousand miles away. And my intact
body is eighteen months paper: the past
a fragile eighteen months regime of trust
in slash-and-burn, in vitamin pills, backed
by no statistics. Each day I enact
survivor's rituals, blessing the crust
I tear from the warm loaf, blessing the hours
in which I didn't or in which I did
consider my own death. I am not yet
statistically a survivor (that
is sixty months). On paper, someone flowers
and flares alive. I knew her. But she's dead.

She flares alive. I knew her. But she's dead.
I flirted with her, might have been her friend,
but transatlantic schedules intervened.
She wrote a book about her Freedom Ride,
the wary elders whom she taught to read,
—herself half-British, twenty-six, white-blonde,
with thirty years to live.
                              And I happened
to open up *The Nation* to that bad
news which I otherwise might not have known
(not breast cancer: cancer of the brain).
Words take the absent friend away again.
Alone, I think, she called, alone, upon
her courage, tried in ways she'd not have wished
by pain and fear: her courage, extinguished.

The pain and fear some courage extinguished
at disaster's denouement come back
daily, banal: is that brownish-black
mole the next chapter? Was the ache enmeshed
between my chest and armpit when I washed
rogue cells' new claw, or just a muscle ache?
I'm not yet desperate enough to take
comfort in being predeceased: the anguish
when the Harlem doctor, the Jewish dancer,
die of AIDS, the Boston seminary's
dean succumbs "after brief illness" to cancer.
I like mossed slabs in country cemeteries

with wide-paced dates, candles in jars, whose tallow
glows on summer evenings, desk-lamp yellow.

Aglow in summer evening, a desk-lamp's yellow
moonlight peruses notebooks, houseplants, texts,
while an aging woman thinks of sex
in the present tense. Desire may follow,
urgent or elegant, cut raw or mellow
with wine and ripe black figs: a proof, the next
course, a simple question, the complex
response, a burning sweetness she will swallow.
The opening mind is sexual and ready
to embrace, incarnate in its prime.
Rippling concentrically from summer's gold
disc, desire's iris expands, steady
with blood beat. Each time implies the next time.
The aging woman hopes she will grow old.

The aging woman hopes she will grow old.
A younger woman has a dazzling vision
of bleeding wrists, her own, the clean incisions
suddenly there, two open mouths. They told
their speechless secrets, witnesses not called
to what occurred with as little volition
of hers as these phantom wounds.
                              Intense precision
of scars, in flesh, in spirit. I'm enrolled
by mine in ranks where now I'm "being brave"

if I take off my shirt in a hot crowd
sunbathing, or demonstrating for Dyke Pride.
Her bravery counters the kitchen knives'
insinuation that the scars be made.
With, or despite our scars, we stay alive.

"With, or despite our scars, we stayed alive
until the Contras or the Government
or rebel troops came, until we were sent
to 'relocation camps,' until the archives
burned, until we dug the ditch, the grave
beside the aspen grove where adolescent
boys used to cut class, until we went
to the precinct house, eager to behave
like citizens . . ."
                        I count my hours and days,
finger for luck the word-scarred table which
is not my witness, shares all innocent
objects' silence: a tin plate, a basement
door, a spade, barbed wire, a ring of keys,
an unwrapped icon, too potent to touch.

TENTATIVE GARDENING

for Nadine George

One November day, with Nadine, whose woods-bound
cabin's an anthology of plantation,
who'd brought over bucket and spade and pitchfork
I laid earth open

for the first time. We planted crocus, iris,
tulip bulbs, for spring, in the strip of garden
I walked out into from my kitchen/mudroom
door in the morning.

Road-ice days, I walked to a neighbor's carport
where Nadine's small Subaru took its shelter
in exchange for having the driveway shoveled
clear by Nadine (who's

had a heart attack and is sixty-seven,
but the neighbor's frail, eighty-three, a widow),
and we'd inch to work through the ice-bedizened
snow-bijou campus

as she'd driven me to twice-monthly chemo
treatments in the dead of Ohio winter
(then we'd go for lentil soup at Ike's truck stop)
nine months before this.

I advised Nadine that a glass or two of
red wine nightly's good for the heart: she knew it
and she savored Juliénas that I gave her
before Thanksgiving.

Blunt Nadine, her iron-gray crop, her gravel
voice, swift limp and straightforward speech, her complex
life pared down to gardening, cats, bilingual
reading: Ohio

made her as cantankerous as our Ovid
on a Baltic coast where they fried in fish oil.
Feminism, faculty cliques, church suppers
didn't include her.

Like James Wright, who learned to drink in Ohio,
I did not think I would grow old there, taking
in stray cats and feeding raccoons, until I
thought I belonged there.

But I did look forward to spring, to thrusting
purple, white, blue, yellow, from green heraldic
leaf spears. I'd plant marigolds for September
after that flowering.

Those bulbs bloomed: March, April. May: my expulsion
happened swiftly. I don't live in Ohio
any longer. Somebody else will see their
secondhand flowers.

Now Nadine's three lines in a crammed address book
(New York, Paris, London, and, yes, Ohio)
and I wonder where and from whom I'll learn to
put in a garden.

A COLLEAGUE

Head in my office, one foot in the hall,
she poised her briefcase—briefly—on a shelf.
"We're all just waiting for the axe to fall.
I ought to have a mammogram myself."

DAYS OF 1994: ALEXANDRIANS

for Edmund White

Lunch: as we close the twentieth century,
death, like a hanger-on or a wanna-be
      sits with us at the cluttered bistro
      table, inflecting the conversation.

Elderly friends take lovers, rent studios,
plan trips to unpronounceable provinces.
      Fifty makes the ironic wager
      that his biographer will outlive him—

as may the erudite eighty-one-year-old
dandy with whom a squabble is simmering.
      His green-eyed architect companion
      died in the spring. He is frank about his

grief, as he savors spiced pumpkin soup, and a
sliced rare filet. We'll see the next decade in
      or not. This one retains its flavor.
      "Her new book . . ." ". . . brilliant!" "She slept with . . ."
        "Really!"

Long arabesques of silver-tipped sentences
drift on the current of our two languages
      into the mist of late September
      midafternoon, where the dusk is curling

★

Just thirty-eight: her last chemotherapy
treatment's the same day classes begin again.
    I went through it a year before she
    started; but hers was both breasts, and lymph nodes.

She's always been a lax vegetarian.
Now she has cut out butter and cheese, and she
    never drank wine or beer. What else is
    there to eliminate? Tea and coffee . . . ?

(Our avocado salads are copious.)
It's easier to talk about politics
    than to allow the terror that shares
    both of our bedrooms to find words. It made

the introduction; it's an acquaintance we've
in common. Trading medical anecdotes
    helps out when conversation lapses.
    We don't discuss Mitterrand and cancer.

Four months (I say) I'll see her, see him again.
(I dream my life; I wake to contingencies.)
    Now I walk home along the river,
    into the wind, as the clouds break open.

INVOCATION

This is for Elsa, also known as Liz,
an ample-bodied gospel singer, five
discrete malignancies in one full breast.
This is for auburn Jacqueline, who is
celebrating fifty years alive,
one since she finished chemotherapy,
with fireworks on the fifteenth of July.
This is for June, whose words are lean and mean
as she is, elucidating our protest.
This is for Lucille, who shines a wide
beam for us with her dark cadences.
This is for long-limbed Maxine, astride
a horse like conscience. This is for Aline
who taught her lover to caress the scar.
This is for Eve, who thought of AZT
as hopeful poisons pumped into a vein.
This is for Nanette in the Midwest.
This is for Alicia, shaking back dark hair,
dancing one-breasted with the Sabbath bride.
This is for Judy on a mountainside,
plunging her gloved hands in a glistening hive.
Hilda, Patricia, Gaylord, Emilienne,
Tania, Eunice: this is for everyone
who marks the distance on a calendar
from what's less likely each year to "recur."
Our saved-for-now lives are life sentences
—which we prefer to the alternative.

BROCELIANDE

for Marie-Geneviève Havel

Yes, there is a vault in the ruined castle.
Yes, there is a woman waking beside the
gleaming sword she drew from the stone of childhood:
hers, if she bore it.

She has found her way through the singing forest.
She has gotten lost in the maze of cobbled
streets in ancient towns, where no lovely stranger
spoke the right language.

Sometimes she inhabits the spiring cities
architects project out of science fiction
dreams, but she illuminates them with different
voyages, visions:

with tomato plants, with the cat who answers
when he's called, with music-hall lyrics, work-scarred
hands on a steering wheel, the jeweled secret
name of a lover.

Here, the water plunges beneath the cliff face.
Here, the locomotive purrs in the station.
Here, beneath viridian skies, a window
glistens at midnight.

GRIEF

for Iva

I

You turned twenty and your best friend died
a week after your birthday, in a car
on a bright icy morning. Now you are
flying home. I called, you called back. You howled; you cried
like the child you probably ceased to be
the moment that I told you she was dead—
your anchor, homegirl, unsolicited
sister.
     Now you are standing in front of me,
tall and in tears and I have nothing to say.
You're too big for me to hold in my skinny arms,
but I do, windbreaker, backpack and all,
stroke snow-splotched wet hair you probably chewed in a storm
of tears in the cab. Your garment bag leans on the wall,
a black dress in it.
           Now I am watching you growing away
from me, toward hours in a car you and two friends drive
through the same treacherous snow, to empty her dorm
room, to sit with the injured boy, wired and re-formed
in plaster, weeping because he was still alive;
toward where you never would have expected to come
to see your friend, or what briefly remained of your friend
thin and naked under a sheet, the wound
at her temple inconsequential-looking (a slight
line of dried blood from her ear) stopped still on a white
marble slab in a crematorium.

I I

Your great-aunts, centenarian-and-some,
write their memoirs. Stroke-silenced, your grandmother
turned eighty in a Brooklyn nursing home,
looking as if she might stand up, recover
her thoughts, her coat, and walk off toward the L
train—though she won't. Chemo has let me live
so far. Some fluke, prudence or miracle
has kept your father seronegative.
The January day they called you out
of computer lab so you could phone
home, I'm sure you ran your cursor down
a list of possible mortalities,
guessing it was death you were called about,
assuming that it would be one of these.

I I I

Your "black dress" was the velvet skirt you wear
for choir recitals. K.J., who stood behind
you at the door, her coat still on, her hands
empty and open, met you at the air-
port, since I was sick. Your grief came in
to us like another illness, one which we
could hardly palliate with soup and tea,
which didn't stop me from making tea again
when I could let you go.

                            But you had gone

farther away, to where she was a light
receding as you watched, to where she was
teasing you on the train to Argelès,
to where she left you at the bus stop ten
days ago, to where she glaringly was not.

I V

I booked you three at the Hôtel Malher:
sixth floor, no bath, a hundred–fifty francs.
You crowded on my couch, made phone calls, drank
tea, took turns showering and washing hair.
You'd had breakfast. You'd gone to the bank.
You were all seventeen. A girl in Tours,
her pen pal, had invited you to come
down for the weekend. You would take the train.
And then you'd take the train to Perpignan.
Was there a train from Tours to Perpignan?
Her mother's (gay) friend had a summer home
in Argelès, had offered the spare room.
(I think I had to route you through Bordeaux.)
You knew your way, some, from years I'd ferried you
over, "Unaccompanied," to France.
She'd spent six exchange months in Budapest,
could be acute about the difference,
but mostly loved the light, the river, under
the influence . . . The boy seemed youngest,
and anything *she* liked, except museums,

he was willing to attest was wonder-
ful too. Like colts, like April trees, your threesome
bristled with innocence and confidence.
A sprained ankle, lost camera, missed train
were the mishaps that you thought to fear.
I sent you out into the summer rain
between your junior and your senior year.

V

A crowd, standing room only, turned out for
her funeral. Masses of wasted flowers
embraced a photo album you'd spent hours
assembling, through the night and dawn, with her
shell-shocked kid sister. Then you'd gone together
to face your first cadaver, and belief
in the obscenity that caused your grief.
The obsequies of a dead senator
might not have brought out such a throng, I said,
standing in line, waiting my turn to view
family snapshots: mother and infant, two-
year-old walking, standing on her head
at eight: domestic Sunday afternoon
pastime turned into mourning. She herself
was now a box of ashes on a shelf
whose sixteen-year-old shadow mugged at you
next to a Beatles poster in your blue
disheveled bedroom as you took that one.

DIRECTIONS

You knew the right title for all these years.
Now the book's in your hands. The book has changed
key, cadence, resonated and resolved strange
dissonances. Days, stanzas disappear,
emerge again, seen otherwise. Yes, we're
hovering over it, translucent, stained
glass saints through whom light filters down, a rain
of colors on an upturned face, in tears
or merely questioning. Or, we're the river
whose motion you can follow through the trees
you look out at on a gray day. A sliver
of light crosses the notebook on your knees
where words dappling the water rearrange
themselves. Outside's the road that brought you here.

Outside yourself, the road that brought you where
you live now disappears into those trees
which disappear, themselves, in fog. The thickening air
makes you think, because you're who you are,
of other woods, in Ukraine, Germany,
Poland, where fog, like anonymity,
hung on bland branches during the massacre.
A continent of disconnected lights
extends in front of you, and then its stark
contours recede. You look at your own hand
—which wields tools, strokes strings, touches a lover, writes—
and close your book, because it's getting dark.
How can you sing their songs in a strange land?

How can I sing their songs in a strange land?
Which river is the river in the song?
Which town was Zion, which was Babylon?
Which language do I still misunderstand
in patches? The FN's in Toulon's
town hall, also in Orange, in Marignane,
while rumors of exclusion are pronounced
daily in flatland mid-American.
The city street's slicked down by the late rain.
It's dim-lit, curtained windows, big as doors,
half-close on half-written biographies
of polyglot and stateless ancestors
whose surnames were folk-tale geography:
golden mountain, vineyard, silver stone.

Goldenberger, Weingarten, Szylberstyn,
had wholesale menswear showrooms on this street
—*maison fondée en mil-neuf-cent-vingt-huit*—
cut and sewed suits in cramped workrooms behind
the shopfronts, or upstairs: noisy, benign
family fiefs. There was one year they cut
and sewed yellow cloth stars. Then the shops shut.
A few returned, repainted their old signs.
Elsewhere, my mother's tailor father, Max
Rosengarten's six workers straggled up
six flights: finishers, pressers, a bookkeeper
—like my father's mother, Gísela
Blau. Now I live above the shop.
A piecework landscape frays behind their backs.

A pieced landscape displayed behind the backs
of saints in blue and scarlet jewel hues
bathes meditative unconverted Jews
with light that pools, prismatic, in the lakes
of votive candles melted down to wax
they lit before they slipped into the pews.
Another generation paid their dues.
The Mass is something like illicit sex.
(They'd have to sit upstairs behind a grille
if their cathedral were the orthodox
synagogue, whose women embroidered this
minute brocaded armchair for a *briss*
they watched from purdah.) On a green glass hill,
some errant ewes observe the docile flocks.

You've errands. You survey the docile flocks
trooping down into the subway in the heat.
(You're glad you work on 22nd Street,
a healthy amble of eleven blocks.)
A hundred books are shrink-wrapped in a box—
like bricks of juice. Bank; druggist's . . . Will you treat
yourself to those new boots? To celebrate
what? It seems pointless, that's the paradox:
a suite of choices as gratuitous
as a coin flipped into a blue chalk
hopscotch grid drawn on cement, which spun
down "lover," "mother," enigmatic "us."
But I'm imagining your morning walk
from the long distance of my afternoon.

From the long distance of my afternoon,
a smell of *frites* comes up from the cafés.
A scruffy jazz group (four French white boys) plays
ragtime beneath the traffic light: trombone,
French horn, sax, banjo. *You're as good as gone,*
you wrote, and went. We live our lives. The day's
muddle of heat condenses in a haze
of car exhaust.
   In whatever time zone
we reach each other cautiously, we touch
in tentatives of words, we frame our fears
with Ashkenazi irony. I keep
that distance—it's the place from which I watched
you, younger, going somewhere in your sleep.
You knew the right direction all these years.

STREET SCENES: SUNDAY EVENING

Flowers at the plinth, curbside, said he wouldn't be back—
a bucket of red tulips, with a sign:
he died the night of February 9th
of cold—hand-scrawled, but worded like a plaque
for an assassinated partisan
"shot here in '42 by the SS."
His friends (it said) are invited to Mass
at the Eglise St-Paul, rue St-Antoine.
He was called Monsieur Guy. The man who lived
there, died under the arches of the Place
des Vosges. We went, remembering him, to the late Mass.
An edgy, bearded man lit white votive
candles, one, then another, dropping five-franc
pieces, his lunch, his breakfast, his next drink,
into the alms box, pacing like a monk
from Mary's candle-lit feet to coin slot. Mink
coats, camels' hair, duffles and anoraks
(on children) clustered in the center pews.
In torn windbreakers and bald running shoes,
the pavement's citizens observed their backs
discreetly. An eighty-year-old woman, whose
face was intelligent as it was clear,
embraced, named, greeted each street person there
to mourn a friend. Couchant beside her, close
to the hem of her neat navy blue
wool coat, a huge Rottweiler cocked black ears
when she (chime-pure) sang, but didn't echo her
responses. Monsieur Guy had a dog too,

a venerable Labrador. Its bed
was blankets in a carton. Mornings, he'd
spit on his handkerchief and swab its eyes.
Thin, lank black hair—both looked wearily old.
"Is that *his* dog?" you asked, meaning the wise
vigilant Rottweiler. Stories I'd told
to you out of the fabric of a day
included them: I'd have passed them on the way
to Sunday market, stood in line behind while he
bought dog food in the late-night Arab grocery.
Once, man and dog reclined against a sun-
warmed wall in August. Monsieur Guy clapped his hands
as an old Japanese couple danced
deft tangos to a street accordion.

The priest referred to wanderers, not sinners,
and the good works of St. Vincent de Paul.
A red-faced woman teetered in the aisle.
We shared handclasps of greeting with the small
street cohort, the bright-voiced dog owner, whose smile
included us. The Labrador is gone,
his friend dead of exposure in the cold,
the evanescent fellowship of one
evening's community hardly recalled
when pious civic families meet old
souls in the street, ragged and reeking wine.
Beside the altar, diffident as beginners,
beside the bucket, with a fresh bouquet,

young street musicians, scrubbed, still dressed in jeans,
grouped in their student string quartet, which plays
under the arches weekend afternoons,
struck up unfunereal Vivaldi
as recessional music Monsieur Guy
(and I) had heard on numberless Sundays.
We went to our respective fasts and dinners.

WEDNESDAY I.D. CLINIC

for K.J.

Your words are ones the patients said themselves.
You carry them inside yourself, their vessel.

The widowed black man with two half-white children might
have given them up, have given up, this time

next month. But you don't say: that woman; this man.
You know their faces. You tell me a first name,

temperament and age, even a T-cell
count, if I ask, which will probably be less

than it was. Not always. Someone bursts into tears.
Someone drags his chair closer, to stare

at you, as if your eyes, your collar, your lips,
said more than that sentence. He asks for vitamin pills.

She asks for condoms. He asks for simpler words.
She shifts the murmuring baby, lets him drowse

against her breast, bounces him on her knee,
starts, almost imperceptibly, to keen

a lullaby, or is it a lament?
As your heart beats, you rock her, in a mental

mutual embrace (you've hugged her) which allows
you to breathe with her, pause with her, swallow

the hard words. She's with you when you come downtown
later. You could keep it to yourself. You won't.

TWELFTH FLOOR WEST

Brandy, who got it from a blood transfusion,
was in for MAC, with a decubitus
ulcer festering. Baffled and generous,
her Baptist sisters brought each day's illusion
that she'd look back at them, that her confusion
would focus into words. They swabbed the pus,
they cleaned the shit, they wiped away the crust
of morning on her lids. The new bruise on
her thigh was baffling. They left an armchair
facing the window: an unspoken goal.
They'd come next morning, find her sitting there
with juice and coffee and a buttered roll.
The day she was released to hospice care
they came to meet her. They held her thin cold
hands on the gurney in the corridor.
The ambulance stood in the bay downstairs.

LONG ISLAND RAILROAD

Outbound

Brown-skinned Manhattan students take the train
east, after the inbound dark-suit commute,
through bleak suburbs built for light industry,

then affluent ones where rows of cherry trees
(through grimy train-car panes and, outside, rain)
in pink bloom now, transform, translate, transmute

anonymous flatland to a landscape's mute
but lively narrative. There are no trees
where workers queue at bus stops in the rain.

Commuters on the train ignore the trees.

Inbound

Stout Long Island Irish boys suck beer
from cans and bottles in brown paper bags.
Basketball season at the Garden's on.

In shiny navy, the conductor, on
her rounds, punches their tickets. Empty beer
cans roll in the aisle. A cooler bag

is stacked with six-packs. Its guardian brags
about a job he might have in construction.
His seatmate pops open another beer.

They bag their beer at Pennsylvania Station.

SQUARES AND COURTYARDS

Across the Place du Marché Ste-Catherine
the light which frames a building that I see
daily, walking home from the bakery,
white voile in open windows, sudden green
and scarlet window-box geraniums
backlit in cloud-encouraged clarity
against the century-patinaed gray
is such a gift of the quotidian,
a benefice of sight and consciousness,
I sometimes stop, confused with gratitude,
not knowing what to thank or whom to bless,
break off an end of seven-grain baguette
as if my orchestrated senses could
confirm the day. It's fragrant. I eat it.

Confirm the day's fragrance. I eat, bit
by bit, the buttery *pain aux raisins*
shell-coiled beside my steaming afternoon
tea. It's the hour for a schoolchild's treat,
munched down, warm in waxed paper, on the street,
or picked at on chipped earthenware (like mine)
beside books marked with homework to be done
while the street's sunlit, dusk-lit, lamplit.
She sucks her pencil, window-framed. I sip
nostalgia for a childhood not my own
Bronx kitchen table, with a fire escape
in the alley shaded by sumac trees
which filtered out the other languages
I heard the airshaft's crosscurrents intone.

I heard the airshaft's crosscurrents intone
below the minyan davening morning offices.
A childish rasp that slurred and sputtered was
the Polish janitor's red-knuckled son
helping his father empty garbage cans.
His voice was why I thought him rough (as is
English when spoken by its novices),
a voice I never heard speaking its own
language. His name was Joseph. He was six.
Other syllables connected news
from gutted Europe to the dusty motes
of Sabbath morning. Ash settled on bricks,
spun up the shaft with voices of old Jews,
was drawn down garrulous chain-smokers' throats.

Drawn up from garrulous chain-smokers' throats
at round tin tables on wet cobblestones
just hosed down by a green-clad African
street cleaner: strikes, prices, who still votes
Left, sex, a sick child. Hands unbutton coats
halfway. The wind's mild, but it looks like rain
above the Place du Marché Ste-Catherine
where charcoal-bellied clouds converge like boats
in the mutable blue harbor sky.
Another coffee, another *blanc sec*—
as if events were ours to rearrange
with words, as if dailiness forestalled change,

as if we didn't grow old (or not) and die
as long as someone listened when we spoke.

As long as someone listened when I spoke
especially someone walking a dog—
I'd launch into juvenile monologue:
Greek myths, canine behavior—and could I stroke
the Lab or spaniel? Speech and touch invoked
my grandmother, the bookkeeper from Prague,
who died as I emerged out of the fog
of infancy, while lives dispersed in smoke
above the camps (and Dresden, and Japan)
and with them, someone else I might have been
if memory braided with history.
I pressed my face into the dog's warm fur
whose heat and smell I learned by heart, while she
receded into words I found for her.

Receding into words I found for her
delight, someone was dispossessed of her own
story (she thought) by mine.
                              Receding in-
to words, the frail and early-rising neighbor
who died during my cancer-treatment year
is not summed up by "centenarian."
Her century requires a lexicon.
I wrote a girl on paper when I bore

a child, whose photocopied life became
letters tattooed across a watermark,
a woman's in the world, who shares her name.
And Gísela, who took me to the park,
for whom I pieced together sentences
—it's all the words she said to me I miss.

It's all the words she said to me I miss,
down to unechoed accents. Did she speak
Yiddish to me? With whom did she speak Czech?
German was what my father spoke till his
sixth year, first grade (when did he tell me this?)
—his parents' common tongue. And did they make
love in their second language? The air's thick
with cognates, questions and parentheses
she'll scribble down once she's back in her room,
chewing her braid, tracing our labyrinthine
fragments. She zips her anorak
and shifts the heavy satchel on her back
watching low clouds gather as she walks home
across the Place du Marché Ste-Catherine.

Not knowing what to thank or whom to bless,
the schoolgirl at the window, whom I'm not,
hums cadences it soothes her to repeat
which open into other languages
in which she'll piece together sentences
while I imagine her across the street

as late light shifts, sunlit, dusk-lit, lamplit.
Is there a yellow star sewn on her dress
as she exults, confused with gratitude,
her century requires a lexicon
of memory braided with history
she'll have reflective decades to write down?
Not thinking, she'll get old (or not) and die;
thinking: she can, if anybody could.

APRIL COUPLETS

for Jenny Factor

Mild sky of a day which may or may not be forgotten
as days of a life, lives themselves, are forgotten.

Tenacious ivy crawls from a plastic pot in
a window-box which the early rain's forgotten.

Nocturnal narrative's coherent plot in
the sleeper's mind disconnects, and the dream's forgotten

textures, flavors, burlap, honey, satin,
systematically derange, dissolve: forgotten.

This morning's crisp half-loaf in which I've bitten
a crescent lies near coffee dregs, forgotten.

On a lined page in front of me are written
haphazard words grasping what I've forgotten.

A letter will be answered today, or not. In
the gap, what it might have said could be forgotten.

A three-year-old picked up a dropped red button
and cried for a lost rag doll not quite forgotten.

The sidewalk glistened in the Marais, Manhattan
or a Balkan town whose vowels howl unforgotten

chronicles of neighbors at war, ill met in
each market-place, blood mixed, but no slur forgotten.

What key turns in the lock, who will be let in
to the bright room of what is not forgotten?

The scribe turns hacker: DOS displaces Latin:
Exiles hoard both, the plain speech of peace forgotten.

AGAIN, THE RIVER

for Geneviève Pastre

Early summer in what I hope is "midlife,"
and the sunlight makes me its own suggestions
when I take my indolence to the river
and breathe the breeze in.

Years, here, seem to blend into one another.
Houseboats, tugs and barges don't change complexion
drastically (warts, wrinkles) until gestalt-shift
dissolves the difference.

Sentence fragments float on a wave of syntax,
images imprinted in contemplation,
indistinct impressions of conversations
which marked some turning.

Food and drink last night with a friend—we've twelve years'
history of Burgundy and good dinners
and as many books off the press between us
toasted together.

Writing is a difficult form of reading.
Paragraphs that roll away from their moorings
seem like passages to another language
half-comprehended.

Sometimes thought is more like a bad translation.
Hazy shapes resistant to sentence structure

intimate—but what do they mean, exactly?
Texture, sound, odor

(dockside, urinous, up on green slopes, roses
in full bloom like elegant girls of forty)
imprint images in aleatoric
absence of order.

Isolated words can unlock a story:
what you ate, she felt when she heard the music,
what's brought back by one broken leaf, whose sticky
sap on a finger

named a green, free season to city children.
Now, daylight's duration is equinoctial:
spring is turning swiftly to summer, summer's
ripeness brings endings.

I can feel a change in the weather coming.
When I catch a glimpse of myself in mirrors,
I see someone middle-aged, with my mother's
sallow complexion.

Who do we write books for—our friends, our daughters?
Last night's dinner companion has two daughters,
women in their thirties with strong opinions.
My child is younger

and might say there won't be books in the "20 . . . s,"
just hard copy downloaded from computers.
Children won't haunt library aisles, as I did,
tracking their futures.

(What about the homeless man reading science
fiction on the steps of St. Paul, a tattered
paperback, a galaxy on the cover
he was approaching?)

Houses are precarious or unsettling.
We who left them young, and applaud our daughters'
rootlessness still scrutinize wind-chapped faces
of pavement dwellers.

"Every woman's one man away from welfare . . ."
he may be a college trustee, a landlord
or a bland, anonymous civil servant
balancing budgets.

My friend's postcard goddesses, morning teapot,
Greek and Latin lexicons, Mac computer
fill the magic cave of a room she works in
which she'll be leaving

when her lease is up (as provincial theater
troops strike sets, pack trunks), lares and penates
ready to be set on a desk and bookshelves
in closer quarters

where she'll reestablish haphazard suppers
on her Cévennes grandmother's round oak table.
Where will I be? Too many airline tickets
away to answer.

(I lead two lives superimposed upon each
other, on two continents, in two cities,
make believe my citizenship is other
than that blue passport's.)

But today there's wind on the Seine; a tugboat
with embroidered curtains and gardened windows
looks like home as it navigates the river
toward other moorings.

TAKING LEAVE OF ZENKA

Rain slants down, crossing out the afternoon;
the roofs slick up, dry out, with cups of tea.
The telephone's adroit cacophony
interrupts what hasn't been begun
and what, again, won't be begun. Connection
to the next scene of a small tragedy.
(*Le Monde's* been in the kiosks since half-past three
working up steam for next Sunday's election.)
In London, Zenka, who is eighty-four,
has colon cancer, and is going to die.
Spilled out, the intellectual champagne
her daily conversation used to pour.
Immobile, she awaits hot soup or pain
or large-print explanations in the sky.

The large-print explanations in the sky
are merely clouds, and what they spell is weather.
The wind resets them; they disperse, or gather
and loose their contents on the passersby.
Tiepolo blue bannered behind the gray
edges diminishing to cotton and feather
mean shower and sunset might occur together
later, this mutable afternoon in May.
The women on the geriatric ward
were mostly not too certain where they were.
One, whose high-cheekboned face had made me stop,
soothed, in that place, by its austere accord,
vomited blankly into her lap
while no one turned around to look at her.

While no one turned around to look at her,
Zenka entranced with wit, mordant and dry,
uncompromising in its scrutiny
of foibles. One could easily incur
a sentence like a briskly shutting door—
but it would open on hilarity
over a lunch of what she'd call a pie
(quiche from Leclerc) and salad; a murmur
of breeze and meridional midday exchange
beyond the terrace. Tough as the transplants
—azaleas and hibiscus—in her garden,
she found the world peculiar, but not strange,
with little she'd condone, and much she'd pardon—
a British Jew who lived in southern France.

A British Jew who lived in southern France
had more than enough history to think
about, lunch dishes piled up in the sink,
her bookshelves groaning, and her common sense
(the roof's been fixed; the dog's been fed; the rent's
not due yet) keeping viable the link
between adventure (eloped—on the brink
of sixty!) and the day-by-daily chance-
taking routine. July, '78: I met
the vivid pair in the ceramics shop
which earned their slender living in Tourrettes-
sur-Loup, on an olive-terraced hilltop.
Tribal (though not initiated yet),
the slightest hint was all I had to drop.

The slightest hint was all I had to drop
to be acknowledged in the family
and hear its gossip: the *salon de thé*
on the town square two "girls" had opened up—
Tourrettes, to hear them, was a *gîte d'étape*
for "ours": the clerk in the *épicerie,*
the gallery, the jewelers . . . Were Marie
and I a couple? Was not asked. I stopped
by the next day, and chose an inkwell, glazed
in opalescent slate, for my singular
friend, who was ill, who is wholly without pair.
We were invited to come back and eat
with them the next evening: such a discreet
acceptance, I accepted, not amazed.

Acceptance I accepted, not amazed
(I was that young) to think that numinous
landscapes, miraculous acquaintances
were in the world for me to seize and praise
(in sentences felicitously phrased).
But if I could adopt my ancestors,
it was because Zenka invented hers:
conceived, accomplished, rehearsed and raised
herself, not losing sight of the East End.
Self-rescued, she became a rescuer
from small ads and suburban oligarchs,
monoglot minds, despotic matriarchs.
Expatriate, she brought the wit to cure
a boyish woman soldier of her wound.

The boyish woman soldier, with a wound
deep now as earth in which a life's interred
shed avian grace, mercurial black bird
on multinational mourners around
the grave, around the hors d'oeuvres where they thronged, beyond
the sliding window to the garden. Blurred
in June fog, North London yellow roses, shirred
peach, bloom where they were planted by her friend.
Slow, but a gentleman in gray, her son,
stumping his crutch, a question, on the floor,
teaches himself absence's rudiments:
"Zenka, in the kitchen, make tea, no more,"
Below the Channel, trains tunnel to France.
Rain slants down, crossing out the afternoon.

RUE DE BELLEYME

Rain from the channel: wind and rain again
umbrellas jostle on the pavement, crowd
together, move apart. Atlantic rain

south from the British Isles. A monocloud
covers the sky that yesterday was blue
and filled with light, where clement winds allowed

expansive breathing, new air flowing through
a sentence or a ribbon or a song
children sang complicated verses to:

a day I could be grateful to for long
light: although not June, still just July
when no direction was entirely wrong

for finding points to take my bearings by
and walk around the corner of a street
that's always there, a small discovery.

If you've misplaced the key, the door is shut
but every street's a door that opens up,
the narrow gangway to a bannered boat:

run up before it raises anchor, slip-
ping otter-like from moorings. On the dock
hands wave bright scarves, and colored pennants flap.

A bus pulled out, a taxi stopped, a truck
parked curbside, the driver undid a latch,
put down a ramp, rolled out a garment-rack.

Two black girls on boot-skates stopped to watch,
dusty from play, homebound at one o'clock
with nectarines and two baguettes for lunch.

(If you've misplaced the key, you're out of luck,
but every window framed another key.
A garden past the crossing winked back black,

copper, gold children to their serious play.)
Sisters, from their matching innocent
navy-blue pleats hemmed short above the knee.

(Somewhere in the next arrondissement
women do piecework in small factories,
mostly undocumented immigrants,

Filipina, African, Chinese,
some of whose children become secular
and republican *lycéens*.) Did these

two with neat ribbons in their cornrowed hair
and roller-skating scabs on their bare knees
memorize La Fontaine and Baudelaire,

and did the rack of one cloned summer dress
with lime-green polka dots and large puffed sleeves
remind them of the end-of-term *kermesse*,

the job their mother hardly ever leaves,
or some preadolescent feminine
world I wouldn't recognize, believe,

or, with the best-intentioned will, imagine?
Their futures opening like a painted fan:
hairdresser, film director, *lycéenne*,

they skated off, one with the nectarines
the other with the loaves under her arm
towards a deserved repast of citizens.

(as I imagined going home with them
the driver, padlocking his empty van,
set off an inadvertent car-alarm)

the lost key in some jacket pocket found
as, equally irrelevant, the rain
clouds open out onto the blue of noon.

LETTER TO MUNNSVILLE N.Y.
FROM THE RUE DE TURENNE

Hayden, my snow field
is this rain-slashed winter street,
worlds behind windows.

Robust old women
and men going to market
pull their wheeled caddies

along the pavement
Sunday morning, as nuns go
to break bread and pray.

Sometimes I'd like to
fade into the market crowd:
shawled, sack of soup greens.

Get rid of the "I"?
One more woman gets on line
at the bakery.

★

Open in an L-
shaped room with two tall windows,
a book of rich hours.

At midnight, full moon
over the rooftops, old friend
from other cities.

Healthy, at fifty
to be apprenticed to an
exigent master.

Where is the dog who
worked at the *Royal Turenne*
till four months ago?

Huge German shepherd,
thick patchy coat, wolf tail, a
frequent erection,

he sat, ears cocked, on
the street, always alert but
discreet with patrons

or lay under a
table, walked himself around
the block in off-hours.

He saw everything
and said nothing: the ground rules
for a café dog:

old dog whose old tricks
kept him faithful at his post
for a dozen years.

And it's a year since
Mme. Magin-Levacher,
ninety, went outside.

★

But the dog's not dead.
He stalks out to the curb, where
a blonde Lab sniffs trash—

a café dog would not
eat garbage! They circle, wag
tails, lope down the street.

The young Antillaise
from the Sécu runs upstairs
with my neighbor's mail.

★

Sixty years ago
knickered Jewish boys played ball
in the Place des Vosges,

sons of socialists
from Galicia, intent on
losing their accents.

Historical fog
shrouds corporeal absence:
a generation's.

Now black-bearded, black-
hatted men cause traffic jams
preaching in the street.

Barred from the chanting,
sweating behind an iron grille,
girls and women pray.

★

January rain
percussive on the panes; then
wind scours the sky blue.

Ice storms paralyze
Québec: winter will be long
across the ocean.

Fat drops glow on the
leaves of wet white primroses
in the window box

★

I've changed the sheets on
the bed I'll sleep in only
another six nights.

A month or six weeks,
three months or four, make a life
in miniature.

Each departure, as
it approaches, reminds me
of the final one.

So I leap ahead
to come back up the four flights
and unlock the door.

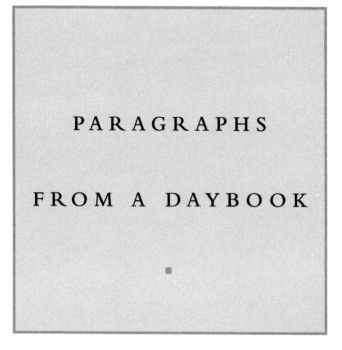

PARAGRAPHS

FROM A DAYBOOK

PARAGRAPHS FROM A DAYBOOK

Filthiest of cold mornings, with the crumbs
of my breakfast *tartine* and the dregs of tea,
to clear away. On the market street the bums,
long-term jobless, stateless, *sans-abri*—
meaning, those without shelter—
crouch on cardboard, wrapped in frayed woolens, filter
out the wind as best they can, discreetly beg:
a plastic bowl beside rag-swaddled legs.
They all are white, and half of them are women.
I talk with one: tall, stained teeth, arched nose and cheekbones
like Norman gentry. She's soft-spoken
as a fifth-grade teacher, who'd have shown
me fluvial maps, and pointed out the human
scale of geography. She huddles down
on the florist's doorstep in the rue St-Antoine.

Her friend camps daily on the Métro stairs,
a tiny skinny woman with blue eyes.
I gave her my old gloves and a blue mohair
scarf when it was five below. Despite her size
and lack of an ounce of fatty insulation,
she vaunts her indomitable constitution
to layered housewives who pass the time of day
with laden caddies, homebound before noon.
In summer, they more or less live on the Quai
Saint-Bernard. The little one strips for the sun
to shorts and a tank top, turning crinkled coffee-brown
around her aster eyes, and looks even thinner,
while her friend tucks a print skirt over her knees and relaxes.
Close to midnight, I sometimes see them sharing dinner
on a plastic plate, on the steps of the Bureau of Taxes.

But it's January now, it isn't summer
and even dog walkers stay off the quais,
while I remain a latecomer
whose own taxes bloat strategies
of empire that bring sitcoms, sneakers, "fast food"
and strident tourists to the neighborhood.
Tired of their solipsistic booming voices,
I walk in parks they don't know. Under bare elms
and maples, Chinese schoolgirls draft their own
fables—homework, after La Fontaine:
a pigeon tells a mallard the advantages
he's gained from learning other languages.
They don't simper when they're joined by boys—is
subservience now merely one of their cultural choices?
"Our" foreign policy chair's Jesse Helms . . .

The topic was "love," and I thought about bound feet;
"how writers invent love with words"—somewhere there is
a trove of "lotus-foot" poems. But how do girls complete
a thought without a word for "clitoris"?
—though there probably is a word meaning "what is cut,"
semantically akin to venom or shit
used when five-year-olds are maimed
with razor blades: that once, it's named.
We think about the things for which we've words;
words tell us what they think of
us, and the paragraph fast-forwards
to a trampled patch of bloody turf
or a kaleidoscope of bright imagination
in which it is possible to focus "love"
without envisaging some mutilation.

In winter, the produce on the stalls
is rufous roots, dark leaves, luminous tubers,
as if earth voided jewels from its bowels
for my neighbors'
Sunday stew pots. Concurrent raucous calls
and odors waft among the vegetables:
merguez sizzles in a skillet, fowl
turn on a row of spits. Damp dogs prowl
between wool-stockinged calves and corduroys.
Tissue-wrapped clementines
from Morocco (gold from old colonies),
salt fish from Portugal and Spain's
olives and oil; cauliflower from Brittany,
also the channel-crossing mist of rain
down from the northwest coast since yesterday.

I almost gushed to my friend about a movie
I'd just seen: the son of a concentration-
camp survivor's homage. Mother tells son
the volumes she remembers. Now she's seventy-
something, tangos in high-heeled elegance
over the abyss of memory.
But we were balancing fine points of translation
with forkfuls of ratatouille in a café
the freezing afternoon of New Year's Eve,
and both of us had other things to say.
Our plates were cleared. With habitual diffidence,
she handed a new manuscript to me
and took (to the Ladies') momentary leave.
I turned a page and read the dedication
to her father, who died at Bergen-Belsen.

For Muriel Rukeyser

Was a woman. Was quixotically prolific.
Was a Jew. Died too young.
Owned up to violence to be pacific.
Unmothered by the words shaped on her tongue,
she chose a child, borne in the aftershock
of her own youth, awakened in world wars.
Her first lover was Republican Spain;
her brothers, the strip miners with brown-lung
disease, brothers for whom
she bore witness, from whom she learned to listen.
Square and dark, she keened outside locked doors,
Homer and Hecuba, woman as epic.
The river of her body was the Hudson,
to which all other rivers brought her back,
an important Jew who died at home.

Thought thrusts up, homely as a hyacinth
wrapped in its bulb like a root-vegetable,
a ninth-month
belly, while the green indelible
pattern's inscribed into the labyrinth.
Thrust into light, it's air's inhabitant
with light and air as food and drink.
A hyacinth, tumescent pink
on the low wooden Mexican chest
confronts the wintry dusk
with informed self-interest.
Leaf spears extravagantly ask
what idea, still gnarled up in a knot
of ganglions, will break through the husk
shaped at last, recognizable as thought.

However well I speak, I have an accent
tagging my origins: that Teflon fist,
that hog wallow of investment
that hegemonic televangelist's
zeal to dumb the world down to its virulent
cartoon contours, with the world's consent:
your heads of state, in cowboy suits
will lick our leader's lizard boots.
My link to that imperial vulgarity
is a diasporic accident:
pogroms in Austria, in Hungary,
the quota, the boat, the apartment
up six cabbagey flights, overtime in the garment
trade, the children fiercely intent
on speaking well, without an accent.

A *Résistant* father died in a concentration
camp. A fifty-year-old father was a prisoner
of war from '39 till the Liberation.
The Germans shot another father
and his mother during the Occupation:
the Breton *maquis* betrayed by infiltration—
collaborators were everywhere.
A grandfather, a grandmother,
both eighty-one, pacifists,
were gunned down by the *Milice*. They
left a note pinned to the old man's chest:
Le juif paye toujours. The Jew always pays.
Their son had shot himself at the end
of the *"drôle de guerre"* in 1940.
These are the absent fathers of my friends.

Trace, on a city map, trajectories
of partially forgotten words
along the river's arteries,
volatile substance of a sentient world.
Mauve heather crowds the window grill. The light
lingers a little later, with a slight
vernal inflection. In a moon-glazed vase
bloom yellow freesias, like some rainy day's
brook bank, in someone else's memory.
Small whirlpools of perception widen, ring
an infant's numinous discoveries
of syllables for animals, toys, trees:
a Lab's thick coat, the dusty birds
in Claremont Park each tardy urban spring,
a stuffed pink leather horse with button eyes.

A question mark in yellow overalls,
I could read. I was three.
I slept with that pink horse. My one doll's
name was V.J. She'd been given to me
to celebrate the Victory
over Japan, that is to say, the Bomb
I'd spend my school days taking shelter from.
I couldn't tie my shoes. But Reddy the fox,
Tootle the engine who jumped off the tracks,
spelled me their stories on my mother's lap
despite weak eyes and poor small-motor skills.
My grandparents were dead: not in pogroms,
not in the camps—of strokes and heart attacks,
merely immigrants, not deportees.
"When you die, does everything just stop?"

Death is the scandal we wake up to, Hayden:
that flash in childhood, then every blue day.
Once conscious of desire, we're laden
with its accountability.
Death and the singer; death and the maiden:
duets you've taken both voices, and played in-
to measured words, their numbers cast-
out lines which lured a shape out past
the lovely bodies which it mimed and praised.
Now the dazzling shape's your own
daughter's in the dance, appalled, amazed,
as sound waves track disaster in the bone.
Futile and gorgeous gestures: words employed
tracking the inconscient revolution
of the wheel whose spokes revolve around a void.

I'm four, in itchy woolen leggings,
the day that I can't recognize the man
down at the park entrance, waving,
as my father. He has ten
more years to live, that spring. Dapper and balding
he walks toward me; then I run toward him, calling
him, flustered by my flawed vision.
Underfoot, the maples' green-
winged seeds splay on mica-specked octagons.
His round face, thin nose, moustache silvered gray
at thirty-eight look (I think now) Hungarian.
I like his wood smell of two packs a day
as he swings me up to his shoulder
and I say, things look blurry far away
—one Saturday, two years after the war.

Grief, pain and sorrow all are *"la douleur,"*
while *"le bonheur"* is simple happiness
which we savored in the hour
seized as the solstice passed
across the heather-misted calendar
whose olive-brown hillocks' December blur
was pierced by the setting sun
as we meandered, *vigneron*
to *vigneron*, well-spring to orchard, stopped
for *Le Monde*, for the view,
pleasure both cumulative and abrupt:
sudden suave vista; beauty we knew
(mist imperceptibly becoming rain)
well enough to recall, while going through
the nuances of sorrow, grief and pain.

Grasp and turn a moment, make it stop,
stand in view, like the freesias in their green
moon with arboreal ribs. A lapsed
monk worked the Burgundian
clay he'd learned, cloistered, to turn and slap,
fire and glaze. While he talked, wet clay dripped
down his bare arms. The moment turns
like clay slip on a wheel, or burns
with sweetness, like the potter's clover honey
offered to us as we
moved with the wrapped box back into the rainy
winter morning. He'd told me he
read Henry Miller, then rethought his vows.
Six months out of chemotherapy,
I heard his daughters singing in the house.

What are the engines of that energy?
A path around a vineyard, sandwiches
and Starbucks' coffee
above the Hudson, a long kiss,
five flights of wooden stairs worn slant by three
centuries' footsteps, an old library
book with bracketed sentences
may make the metamorphosis
to firm words from memory's shift and slip
the way the moistened clay
turned and handled on the wheel whirled up
and swelled into the belly of a vase,
and curved out to the flower-implicit lip—
the movement is the potter's, not the clay's:
a flaw, and he aborts it with a slap.

Wednesday night at the Comédie Française:
a hundred (white and slender) well-behaved
adolescents, from one of the good *lycées*,
file into balcony rows saved
for them to see Genet's
"Les Bonnes."
            We're older than the actresses,
one of whose roles I took on
in San Francisco, our "salon
production"—two men and one woman,
in black shirts and tight
black jeans. I was "Madame"
for my friends' lyric vengeance five Friday nights.
Gerry, our "Solange," delivered her
last monologue, hands crossed, bald under the rigged spotlight,
like a condemned man awaiting the executioner.

James's gentle philologic daftness led
him to invent a language and its people,
both called "Prashad"
cognate with Slavic "Truth," simple and supple
enough for gnomic folktales. He had
written their history, which filled four hundred
typed pages, and three short plays
which we three, fresh from Genet's
ceremonies, undertook to memorize
and then, to perform.
I was a fag-hag in my early twenties;
shared with my friends their thrift-shop retro charm
and the facility of a linguist
for recitations in dramatic form
in a language that didn't quite exist.

But James died youngish, twenty years ago
and Bill, who played "Claire," my friend then, doesn't speak
or write to me (still from San Francisco)
because I wrote a book
he didn't like. We shared a vast bay-windowed
flat with Paul (Chip, sometimes). Bill lives, now,
alone in a room at the "Y"
from which he goes to work every day
and returns, a wall away from homelessness.
In our rundown wooden
Victorian south of Market, east of Van Ness,
a trestle table in the kitchen
seated ten for feasts provisioned at
a cut-rate market called "The Dented Can."
No—it was Bill and I who named it that.

And Bill and I imagined lives in France
where he had sojourned as an army brat
while I had merely a Romance
Language degree. Often, we sat
among Paul's convalescent kitchen plants
gossiping avidly, with flawed accents,
over coffee mugs and *pan
dulce* from the Mexican
grocery next door.
                                Tunisian
Jews have a new snack bar downstairs
featuring bagels and American
soft drinks, favored, it appears,
by Sunday shoppers in the neighborhood
where I've lived these past twelve years,
decades eclipsed, accent somewhat improved.

My life ago, in this renascent slum
shabby Jews in sweatshops, with irregular
papers, wherever they came from,
gathered midmorning around a samovar
enthroned amidst rows of Singer sewing machines.
They trusted the Republic. They were last seen
being beaten with rifle butts onto sealed trains.
Their great-nephews are Orthodox extremists;
their great-nieces are hash-smoking anarchists.
Some of the sweatshops are high-priced oak-beamed flats,
but I live in one of their tenements
with smeared hallways, corroded pipes, centenarian drains
and five flights of ancient, patinaed spiral stairs
getting junk mail from clothes jobbers and bureaucrats,
sheltered from fascists and the elements.

When I've described my life like this, I've lied.
I also live in six airy rooms on upper Broadway
just south of Harlem, which I bought when my mother died
—a schoolteacher whose penury
left me the wherewithal for bedroom windows
with a view, two long blocks west, of the Hudson.
One friend thinks I'm a coddled American
hypocrite after she spent ten days with me there:
America, whose deep thumbprint of blood's on
cachectic brows from the Bronx to Zaire.
Addicts with AIDS warehoused in SROs
hidden on sidestreets south of Riverside
Drive might not find Kosovo
or Kigali on a map, but tonight, they know
people like them will starve and freeze somewhere.

—which is Saturday night, so that's where my lover
is, giving out condoms and clean syringes
door to door, floor to floor. Someone's had fever
for a week. She's shown an abcessed sore. Nobody scrounges
quarters or cigarettes.
                              Some rooms are neat.
Their tenants ask her in. There's a hot plate,
a kettle, pictures of cats from a magazine
taped to the wall. She sits on the chenille
bedspread, and hears about the son, fourteen,
who lives with his grandmother outside Asheville.
There are some rooms she'd rather not go in.
                                                  Her

colleagues, two medical students and a nurse,
each with a backpack and a sharps container
come down the stairs from the upper floors.
                                        Of course
she knocks on those doors, and goes in, when she's asked in.

At nine or so, she's done, and there's a table
set, amber liquid threading ice,
a cork drawn, bread broken, companionable
alto spirals, pulsed by the bass;
on the street, slang and sirens of upper Manhattan.
Robert is dead, and Melissa, and Geraldine,
Larry, Angel. Doris started Crixivan.
So did Wilhelmina. They're both in wheelchairs.
The grainy blowup on a gallery
wall—a man slumped onto a leatherette
sofa, eyes open, pupils rolled back: dead
is snapshot legacy or prophecy.
The smart-ass golden boy photographer,
Kevin, who started the needle exchange from his van
died in his living room of an overdose.

It's hot for May. The woman hugs the wall
beside the doorstep of the dry cleaner,
cup at her feet, face ruddy, as it al-
ways is, outdoors summer and winter.
Most likely this is due to "alcohol,"
though I have never seen her and her girl-
friend with so much as a bottle
of *pinard*. Wild Nights! Or unsubtle
dawns when only stupor permits sleep.
It will probably turn cold
and wet again, gray damp will slip
down like lichen on the old
pilings where perpetual houseboats moor.
We exchange morning greetings, her controlled
survival smile, my ritual coin, *"bonjour," "bonjour."*

His ex, Eddy, will smoke up what's left to steal.
José is dead, of PCP pneumonia:
third bout, three weeks in hospital.
They both lived in the Hotel California,
a seventies song title, not at all
like the seventies, except in its surreal
aspect; cocaine and heroin
also something in common.
Every dry day, José sold used books
from a table on Broadway.
While a couple, they had houseplants, six cats, cooked
arroz con pollo on a hot plate; José
fixed up found bicycles he carried in:
transient objects which will drift away
into the next binge of his next of kin.

Daily she traverses the frontiers
health/sickness; sheltered/outcast; life/death:
doorways on dingy corridors,
sentences with pits dug underneath
them, the eloquence of absence or
presence (in from the street to wait for her).
Home, tired, she calls her friend,
gets the machine. The phone rings, and
it's not a patient with his viral load
and T-cell count come back
from the lab. Her friend is dead
at forty, of a heart attack.
Minutes ago, on tape, the alto voice
solicited her message with a joke.
Dinner tomorrow night? Or brunch? Your choice . . .

An almost-empty Air France afternoon
flight to New York
(booked the same morning in the rue Caron
travel agency) carried me back
like a rich cousin, for a long weekend.
I thought about how frequently a plane
returned me to somebody's bed,
evoking desire instead
of the body as locus of loss.
Caresses once reminded me
of touching that palpable mass
in my breast, touching mortality.
Though now I count back years away from that
there's still a dismal kind of irony
that I'm here on this last-minute flight.

The heavy presence of so much raw grief;
the oddness of my being there in June;
the way she worked at it inside herself
the way a dog worries an open wound:
the ruined skin open, the thick pelt stiff
with blood, not knowing why it tastes like this.
I'd say, I'd salve, but I'm useless
in her corporeal distress.
I can't make this a normal Friday night:
a film, a meal, although she goes
along with it. We saw a movie, ate
as couples on Columbus Avenue
still stopped, at half-past-ten, to window-shop
the Birkenstocks and Kenneth Cole dress shoes,
the sherbet-colored T-shirts at The Gap.

What I remember of the seventies
in London: carpeted hallway stairs, red bars
of an electric fire, neat whiskey
downed in chilly book-strewn interiors;
grime-paned French doors opening out on
a Hampstead garden greened with daily rain;
a round table Vermeered in rugs;
lukewarm coffee in chipped mugs;
the inexplicable sobriety
attendant upon sexual anarchy;
unfiltered Gauloises I inhaled—they stung
and rendered me expansive, like the drink;
last night's dishes stacked in everyone's sink.
Expatriated from the child I'd been,
it didn't occur to me that I was young.

No more Lysol, only lavender
within the brick suburban garden wall
evoked Zenka in its summer odor
of her savored meridional
years, as we traded anecdotes of her
flight from damp British Junes, in which we were
sharing the "funeral baked meats."
Golden July in '78—
(I tell an Englishwoman I've just met)
remembering the new-
bloomed azure of the sky above Tourrettes
where the brave, definitive two
glazed a choice I had already made
with lavender and olive, gold and blue.
This is their London garden. One is dead.

Two funerals in June, in two
countries, in one week.
Death has a tendency to overdo
and life to border on the bathetic.
In Paris, nobody that I know
is dying. The days unwind, a slow
ribbon toward midsummer. It rains
intermittently. No trains
or planes scheduled, I put my things in order.
New passport stampings mark
the week of my, Ellen's and Zenka's border
crossings, unplotted flight-paths towards the dark.
My mind flings itself toward tranquility:
the Chinese girls turn cartwheels in the park
on the rain-lush *pelouse autorisée.*

A snapshot, after all, is a *cliché*:
so shatter and dazzle, oil on water. Spread like oil
in feather spirals, lapis lazuli,
viridian, crinkled foil,
amethyst, the heart of the crystal. Be
elsewhere, anywhere, synchronicity
irrelevant as a metronome.
Be out to lunch. Be at home
to irony, icons, iconoclasts.
The windows float, opaque
on late afternoon light that lasts and lasts
keeping an errant mind awake
through the arousal of an appetite
for love no one remembers how to make
last, in the close proximity of night.

Cherry-ripe: dark sweet *burlats*, scarlet *reverchons*
firm-fleshed and tart in the mouth,
bigarreaux, peach-and-white *napoléons*
as the harvest moves north
from Provence to the banks of the Yonne
(they grow *napoléons* in Washington
State now). Before that, *garriguettes*,
from Perigord, in wooden punnets;
afterwards, peaches: yellow-fleshed, white,
moss-skinned ruby *pêches de vigne*.
The vendors cry out "Taste," my appetite
does, too. Birdsong, from an unseen
source on this street-island, too close for the trees:
it's a young woman with a tin basin
of plastic whistles moulded like canaries—

—which children warbled on in Claremont Park
one spring day in my third year. Gísela
my father's mother, took
me there. I spent the days with her
now that my mother had gone back to work.
In a brocade satchel, yarn and needles, a picture book
for me. But overnight the yellow bird
whistles had appeared
and I wanted one passionately.
Watching big girls play hopscotch at curb's edge
or telling stories to V.J.
under the shiny leaves of privet hedge
were pale pastimes compared to my desire.
Did I hector one of the privileged
warblers to tell us where they were acquired?

—the candy store on Tremont Avenue.
Of course I don't call her *Gísela*.
I call her Grandma. "Grandma will buy it for you,"
—does she add *"mammele"*
not letting her annoyance filter through
as an old-world friend moves into view?
The toddler and the stout
gray-haired woman walk out
of the park oval toward the shopping streets
into a present tense
where what's ineffaceable repeats
itself. Accidents.
I dash ahead, new whistle in my hand.
She runs behind. The car. The almost-silent
thud. Gísela, prone, also silent, on the ground.

Death is the scandal that was always hidden.
I never saw my grandmother again.
Who took me home? Somebody did. In
the next few days (because that afternoon
and night are blank) I don't think I cried. I didn't
know what to ask (I wasn't three), and then I did, and
"She's gone to live in Florida" they said
and I knew she was dead.
A black woman, to whom I wasn't nice,
was hired to look after me.
Her name was Josephine—and that made twice
I'd heard that name: my grandmother's park crony
was Josephine. Where was Grandma; where was Gísela,
she called me to her bench to ask one day.
I say, "She's gone to live in Florida."

On a beechwood sideboard, there sat in state
an object whose functional equivalent
would be, in American, a trivet,
but "trivet" originally meant
something three-legged—no, that isn't it.
A recollection that I can't translate:
carved wood, a blue ceramic square,
chimes which a child with short brown hair
released into the air, turning a key,
on a noon-shuttered kitchen's red-tiled floor.
The still heat of the estival Midi
exhaled, leonine, beyond the door
as the child, bare-legged and barefoot,
made up verses for
the tune she'd conjured out of the hot plate—

—if that's the word for it.
A gray June afternoon outside Auxerre,
the last few tables of a flea market:
on one of them, boxlike, carved wood, a square
tile, with fin de siècle bathers, set
in it, a key between its four squat feet
which I turn. "Für Elise"
chimes in the dusty marketplace.
And somehow I participate
in a midsummer memory
of a cool moment, a still neutral date.
The thin child, a large scab on her right knee,
stands in the shuttered midday darkness, while
I hold what's entered my own history:
music; carved wood, a blue ceramic tile.

She shuns her dead friend's doorway with a brief
unnecessary detour; jaywalks south.
An eighth-floor window gleams as if . . .
From his hand to the page's mouth
a black streak of illuminated grief
follows the current of a daughter's life.
Nothing will restore these young women.
Nor do we know when it will come.   In
his stove-lit snow-walled cabin, the bereaved
father stubs out a cigarette.
In what vouchsafed grief-years will he have grieved
adequately?   She will forget
sometimes, when the phone rings, who it might
be, and who it is not.
She will remember how it rang that night.